YOU… IN BALANCE

Pat Quinn

PACIFIC LEARNING

www.pacificlearning.com

CONTENTS

1. AN AMAZING MACHINE

Your body is an amazing machine. It has many parts that work together to help you walk, talk, eat, play, learn, and grow. Even when you're asleep, your body is busy doing things, such as making new **cells** and **digesting** food.

Some Amazing Parts

The human body is made from billions of cells. These make **organs**, muscles, bones, **nerves**, skin, and hair. Your brain, which is one of the largest organs in your body, has twelve million cells.

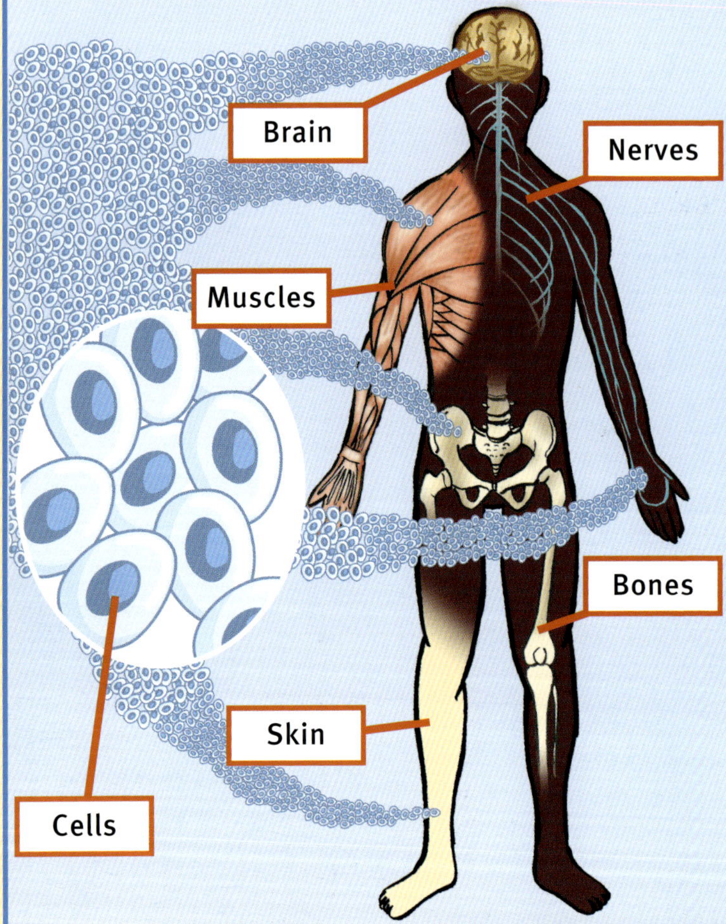

Your heart is another important organ. It pumps blood around your body through 60,000 miles (97,000 kilometers) of tiny tubes called blood vessels. Blood carries food, water, and oxygen to your cells.

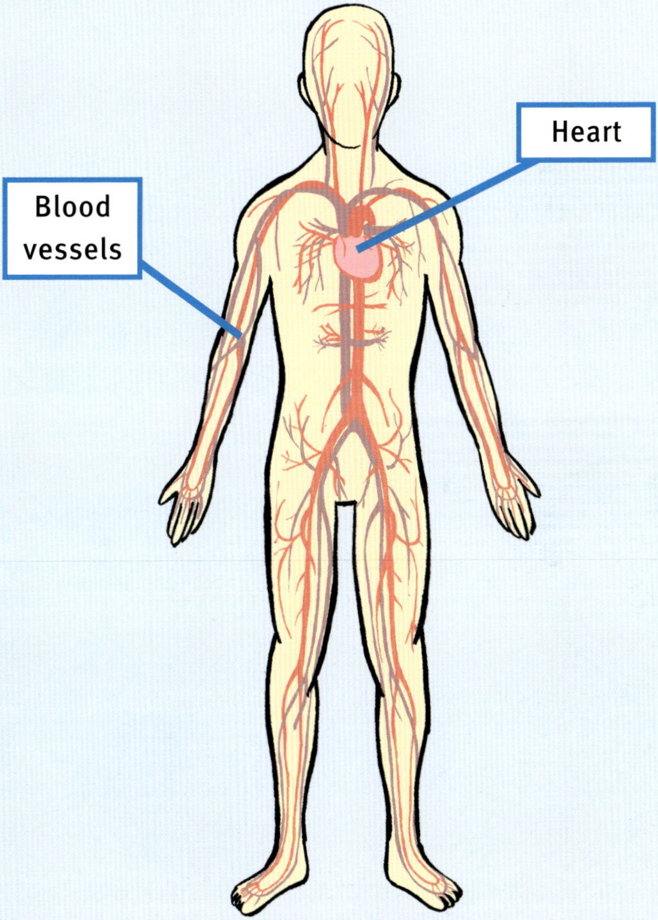

Your body needs four important things to work well: food, water, exercise, and sleep. If you don't get enough of these, you probably won't feel healthy. If you get too much of them, you might not feel healthy either! Your body needs the right balance of food, water, exercise, and sleep so that it can work properly.

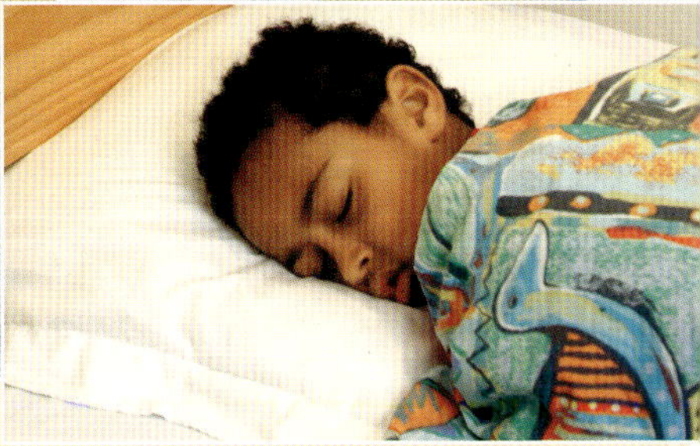

Oxygen

Before you can eat, drink, exercise, and sleep, your body needs one more important thing – oxygen. All living things must have oxygen to survive.

Oxygen is a gas that's found in the air around us, and it's needed by every cell in your body. Cells use oxygen to burn food and turn it into energy. You breathe oxygen through your nose or mouth and into your lungs. The oxygen then passes into your blood and is carried to your cells.

Most people breathe in and out between fourteen and sixteen times a minute. After exercise, this can be as much as sixty times.

2. FOOD

Food is fuel for your body, just like gasoline is fuel for a car. Food helps your body to grow and stay healthy.

Eating food gives you energy so that you can do things, such as walking, making your bed, or doing homework.

How does your body tell you it needs food?

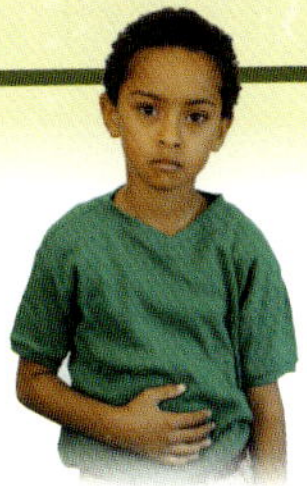

You feel hungry. Your stomach feels empty or makes gurgling noises. When you think about food, your mouth makes **saliva**.

Most people eat around 35 tons of food during their life. That's enough to pack seventy large cars with groceries!

STEP-BY-STEP

What Happens When You Eat?

1. Your teeth grind the food and mix it with the saliva in your mouth. This helps the food to slide down your throat and into your stomach.

2. Special juices in your stomach begin to digest the food. It then passes into your small intestine.

3. **Nutrients** from the food pass through the walls of your small intestine and into your blood.

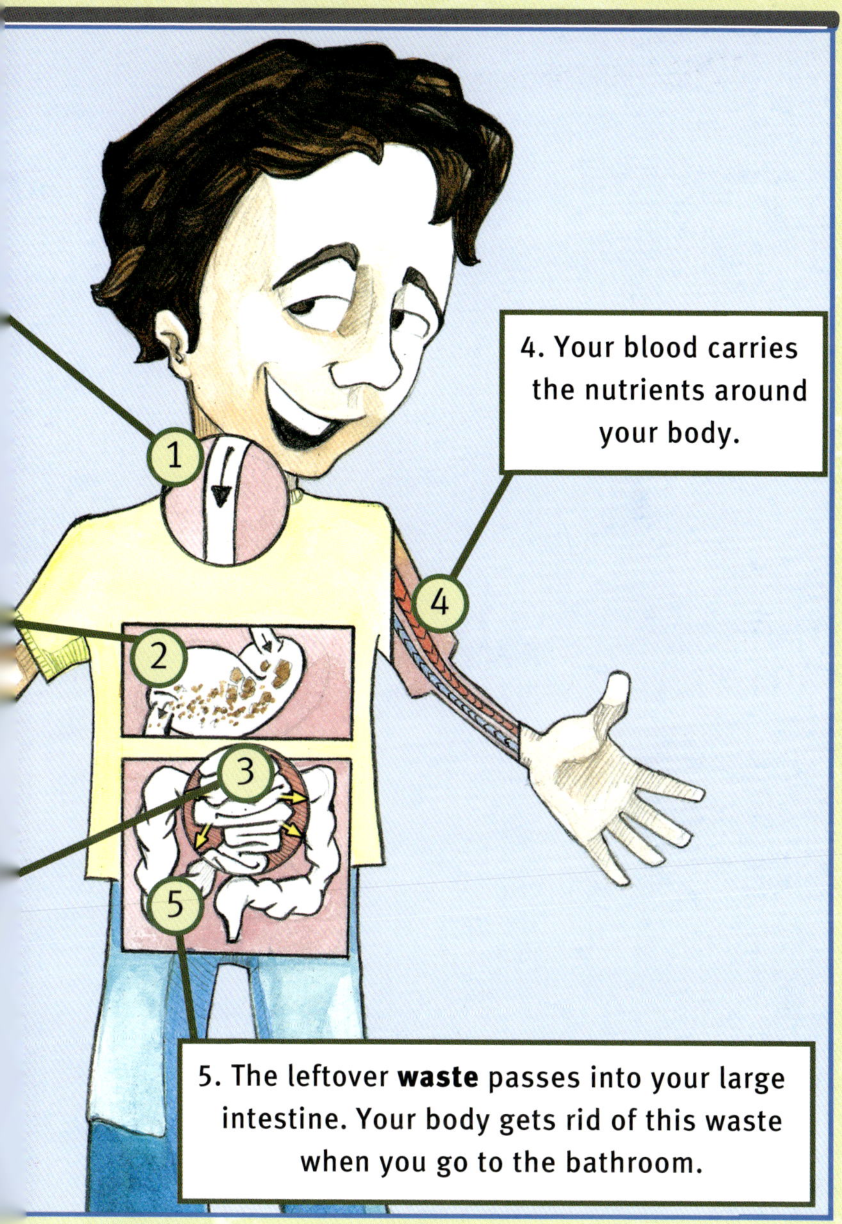
1
2
3
4
5
4. Your blood carries the nutrients around your body.
5. The leftover **waste** passes into your large intestine. Your body gets rid of this waste when you go to the bathroom.

Your body needs a regular supply of food. If you don't eat enough, it will run out of fuel and not work properly.

If you don't eat regularly, you won't have much energy, and you may feel tired or sick.

If a person eats too much, their body will have more fuel than it needs and will store the extra energy as fat. When a person often eats too much, they can become **overweight**. This can make them feel sick and tired, too. It's important to eat the right amount of food – not too little and not too much.

A Balanced Diet

It's important to eat a balance of foods so that your body gets all the things it needs. This is called a balanced diet. To have a balanced diet, we need to eat food that contains proteins, carbohydrates, fats, vitamins, and fiber.

	Main job	*Found in*
Proteins	Build and **repair** muscles and bone	Meat, fish, beans, nuts, eggs
Carbohydrates	Give energy	Bread, rice, cereals, pasta, potatoes, and some fruit
Fats	Give energy	Oil, butter, cream
Vitamins	Help the body work well	Vegetables, fruit, meat, fish
Fiber	Helps with digestion	Vegetables, fruit, beans, and grains

3. WATER

Every living thing needs water to stay alive – and that includes people! More than half of your body is made from water. Very young children have even more water in their bodies.

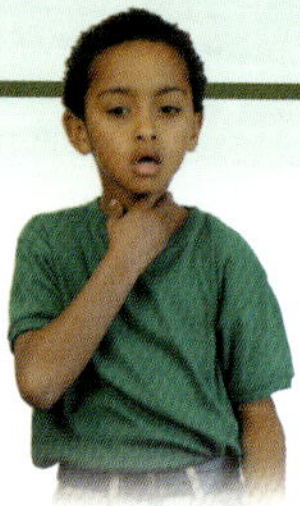

How does your body tell you it needs water?

You feel thirsty, and your mouth feels dry. You'll probably feel hot or tired. You might have a headache.

Most people need to drink between six to eight glasses of water a day to stay healthy. On hot days or when you're exercising, you should drink even more. This is because your skin makes sweat to cool your body, and sweat is mostly water. Your body also loses water when you go to the bathroom to pass **urine**.

LOOKING CLOSER

Water and You

Around 60 percent of your body is made from water. The parts of your body that contain a lot of water include:

- blood, which carries oxygen and nutrients around your body and takes away waste.
- **mucus** in your nose, mouth, throat, and stomach. Mucus is the slimy stuff that helps to trap the things we breathe in, such as dust and germs, and keeps them from entering your lungs.
- digestive juices in your stomach and small intestine, which contain chemicals that break down food.
- muscles, which allow your body to move and help your organs to work.
- bones, which make your skeleton and support your body. Bones also protect your organs and help you to move.

Each of these parts needs plenty of water so that it can work properly.

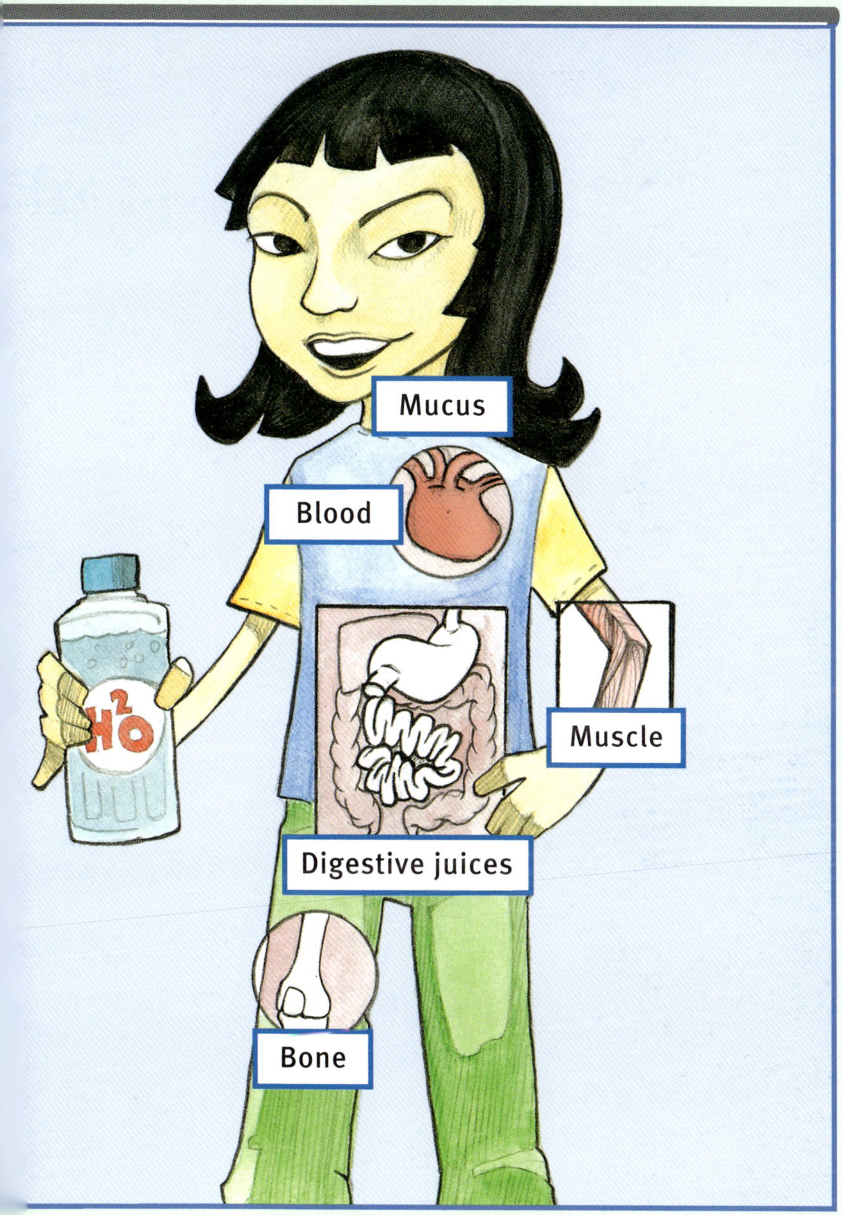
H2O
Mucus
Blood
Muscle
Digestive juices
Bone

Food also contains water. Some foods have a lot of water, especially oranges, melons, grapes, lettuce, cucumbers, and celery.

Some animals that live in dry places get water from eating cactuses.

How much water is in the food you eat?

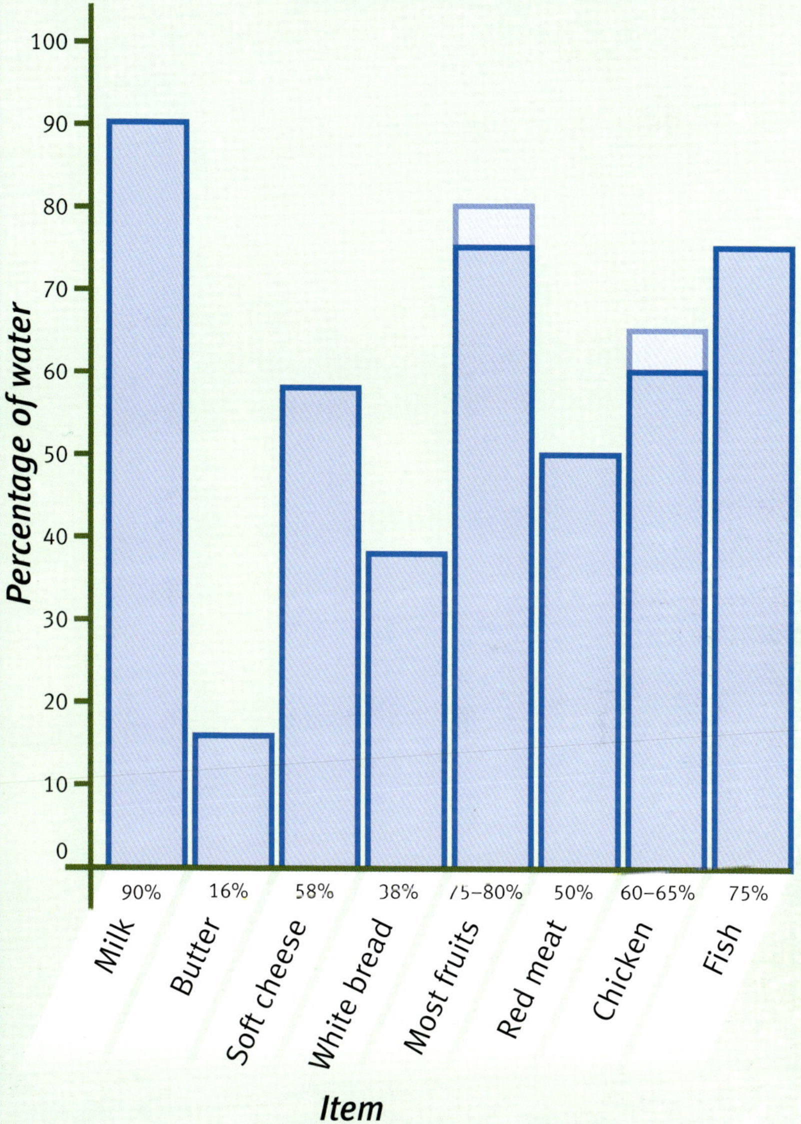

4. EXERCISE

When you eat the right kinds of food in the right amounts and drink plenty of water, your body will feel great. To keep healthy and stay in shape, you also need to exercise.

How does your body tell you it needs exercise?

You feel sleepy or restless. You are easily winded. You might be putting on weight.

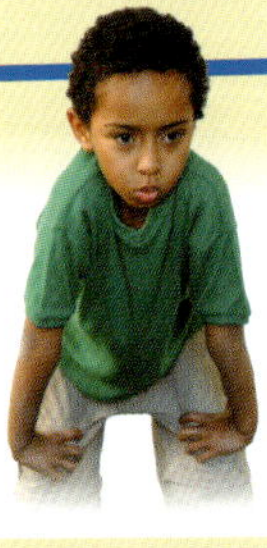

There are two kinds of exercise. Some people like to play a sport, swim, jog, or ride a bike. These activities make you breathe more air, and this makes your muscles work better – especially your heart. This kind of exercise also helps to burn extra fat, which keeps a person from becoming overweight.

Some people like doing exercise that makes their bodies stronger. They might lift weights or do push-ups for a short time each day.

WEIGHING BOTH SIDES

Enjoying Exercise?

Some people find exercising difficult, especially if they're not in shape. They may worry about doing an exercise in the wrong way and hurting themselves. They may also prefer to do other things.

Other people like exercising because it makes them feel healthy and gives them energy. Sometimes exercise or playing a sport can make a person feel good about themselves, especially if they play a sport well. They may also enjoy being outdoors and spending time with other people.

After a day of food, water, and exercise, your body is ready for another important thing ... sleep.

5. SLEEP

Sleep may not seem as much fun as eating, drinking, and exercising, but it's just as important. While you sleep, your body gets ready for the next day.

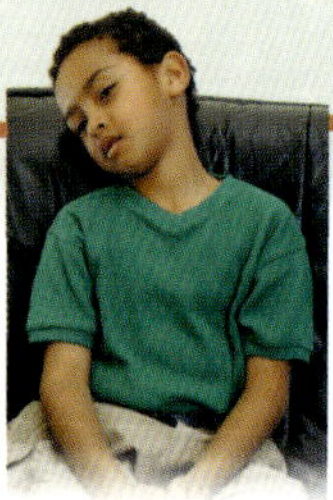

How does your body tell you it needs sleep?

You feel tired and sleepy, and you keep yawning. You can't concentrate. Your eyelids begin to close …

Children need more sleep than adults – usually around ten hours each night. If you don't get enough sleep, you'll probably feel tired and grumpy. When you're tired, things that are usually easy to do become more difficult. Sleeping too much can make you tired as well! It also means you have less time to do other things.

While you're sleeping, your heart beats more slowly and your muscles relax. However, your brain is still working, and this is when you dream.

Even though we dream, we don't always remember what we dream about. Some people think dreams are just stories our brains make up and they have no meaning. Others think that dreams can tell us more about ourselves.

How much do they sleep?

	Animal	Hours of sleep each day
	Giraffe, elephant, horse, sheep, cow	2–4
	Pig, chimpanzee	8–10
	Dog, duck, rabbit, dolphin	10–11
	Cat, rat, mouse	12
	Squirrel, tiger	15–16

Although we look different from one another, our bodies need the same things. Food, water, exercise, and sleep in the right amounts will help to keep your body in balance.

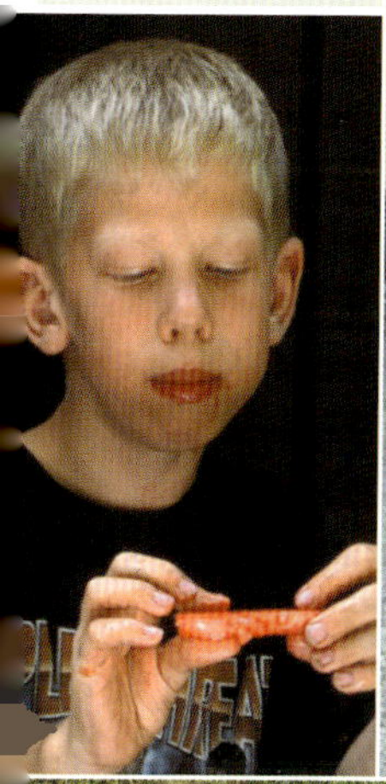

GLOSSARY

(These words are printed in bold type the first time they appear in the book.)

cell: a tiny part of a living thing

digest: to break down food so that the body can use the nutrients (see below)

mucus: a sticky liquid that traps dirt and germs and keeps some parts of the body from drying out

nerve: a part of the body that carries messages from the brain

nutrient: something found in food that helps the body to grow

organ: a part of the body such as the brain, heart, kidney, liver, and lungs

overweight: when the body has too much fat

repair: to fix something

saliva: the liquid made in the mouth to soften food

urine: the liquid the body gets rid of when a person goes to the bathroom

waste: something the body doesn't need anymore

INDEX